MW00736480

BEAUTIFUL RUSH

Marc Vincenz

For Alec,
From an
"upon-a-star
shopping spree...!
in friendship"
JC.

JC Cambridge
October 2017

Unlikely Books

www.UnlikelyStories.org

Beautiful Rush
Winner of the 2013 *Unlikely Mississippi* Prize
Poems Copyright © 2014 Marc Vincenz
Cover and Interior Art Copyright © 2014 Inga Maria Brynjarsdottir
Cover: "Moth"
Book Design Copyright © 2014 Unlikely Books

All Rights Reserved

ISBN-13: 978-0-9708750-2-0

Unlikely Books
www.UnlikelyStories.org
PO Box 2794
Lafayette, LA 70502

Second Printing

—for Terra Incognita

ADVANCE PRAISE FOR *BEAUTIFUL RUSH*

"Marc Vincenz's *Beautiful Rush* is a vertiginous read, a spellbinding, fascinating new poetry collection exploring 'the rapture of being alive' and 'murmuring / ancient bone music, / skin songs / and marrowed incantations.' Sophisticated, profound and inventive, it awakens the reader to a wildly intriguing journey encompassing beauty, presence and absence, death, ghosts, memories and dreams, ecstasy and nothingness. Written with incisive and confounding intelligence, wit and impertinence, 'with the blood of wilderness,' *Beautiful Rush* transports us to 'the marvels / beyond time straight / into the face / of a dimmed / inarticulate world' and 'the color / of pure silence— / that rainbowed tint / when night swallows reflections.'"

– Hélène Cardona

"To 'write an ode at all,' one speaker laments, in Marc Vincenz's *Beautiful Rush*, which 'sings the song of the world' as it guides us along the 'peach-and-velvet-petal road' of its gorgeous, philosophical investigations into 'the birthing of suns,' nights 'of excess,' 'shimmering gold' skies, 'war scars,' 'crab-apples of misfortune,' 'ancient bone music,' and 'the blood of wilderness.' Every poem is a celebration, an exaltation of the 'potential for chaos' amidst the 'rapture of being alive.' Thus, Vincenz accomplishes the task—in *Beautiful Rush*, he has written a multilayered, multi-voiced, and meticulously examined 'ode to Beauty.' Read it, and wonder at the world again."

– Molly Gaudry

Marc Vincenz is one of the finest poets of his generation and has an uncanny ability to register the most subtle shifts of human interaction."

– Katia Kapovich

"What gorgeous poems Marc Vincenz has written. He speaks to us in a sensual, vivid, and measured eloquence. You may flinch at times as his

poems do their work—or you might be thoroughly delighted by an image, or a beautifully assessed line. Either way, you will leave this book feeling utterly invigorated."
– Yussef El Guindi, winner of the Steinberg/ American Theater Critics Association's New Play Award

"Let the reader find truth and heed the Cassandra warnings of our age, mad though they may appear. In *Beautiful Rush*, Marc Vincenz invokes the spirit of Cassandra, Simenon, H.G. Wells and others to make prophetic and finely tuned poems, modern yet compelling as the ancient curse poems of classical times—so that we, in Vincenz's words, 'never / turn out the light / on the wilderness /of our future.'"
– Morgan Harlow

"In *Beautiful Rush* Marc Vincenz conjures a grand, old lyrical voice, sometimes the result of deliberate imitation and here and there punctuated by contemporary irreverence. This voice encompasses romantic love, love of the particular, and (our current bogeyman) gestures toward the universal. Vincenz has delivered a tightly crafted and overwhelming book."
– Hugh Tribbey

"In *Beautiful Rush*, Marc Vincenz marries the inexorable passage of time to its polar opposite, beauty; to the ephemeral 'fragrance of significant things.' This is a collection of generous, tender lyrics, of 'ancient bone music,' a powerful read."
– Lynne Thompson

"Marc Vincenz' poems are edgy, fresh, well-crafted and moving. The voice behind the poems is skeptical, if not cynical, while its shadow between the lines is poignant with the pain of living now. Wielding the 'fine toothed comb of perception,' Vincenz, particularly in the series called 'Beautiful Rush,' which is woven throughout the book, allows us to experience the mystery of his journey, its doubts, its occasional epiphanies."
– Gail Entrekin

"Does the death of a daughter mean naught? *Beautiful Rush*, Marc Vincenz' fifth collection, is haunted by the muse of Cassandra: the speaker acts as witness to her alienation and burden of debt ('your neck . . . Prodded / with a loan shark's knife'), an empathy attenuated by his own scientific ratiocinations as 'other' ('What's it like / to be the victim?') and offset by his own poetic and anthropologic labor ('silent grave-digging / for antediluvian bones, for crude evidence / of concerned mammals . . . and those unrepeating, / unrepeating worlds'). The burden of proof Vincenz frames first as beauty, titularly and in 'ode to beauty,' yet ultimately, as this book is scored by the hunt for truth (however impossible, as were Cassandra's words), not comfort, its speaker finds peace in the liminal, before acquiescing to the arrival not of Venus in Furs but a voice speaking in a language we are finally prepared to receive: 'you hear voices / in hard labor, / and behind closed rooms…something / like knowledge, clearing its throat.'"

– Virginia Konchan

""Marc Vincenz's latest collection, *Beautiful Rush,* provides a modern take on the sublime, leading his readers to the edge repeatedly—to coastlines, sure, but also to ghosts and galaxies. The mortal and immortal live side by side in these poems, nowhere more evident than in the meditations on Cassandra and Simenon, goddess and writer. Elsewhere, cartilage appears next to suns, a broken nose by epiphany. It's easy to imagine this book 'smoking out / the origin of stars.' Vincenz's poetry has that kind of confidence, hard-won and believable, even as the lines embrace what is unknown in 'a dimmed / inarticulate world.'"

– Erica Wright

THE ORDER IN WHICH THEY APPEAR

FOREWORD

"Ears open, I wanted so much to listen." If, as Heschel said, the prophet is one who *employs notes one octave too high*, then Vincenz has transcribed what he has heard—including "ancient bone music, / skin songs / and marrowed incantations"— so that we can listen in. Vincenz is attuned to what most of us miss in "the song of the world." He listens until he hears "something / like knowledge, clearing its throat" and beyond that, in "a vast underground of pure silence," also "a language called stillness" beneath our human babble.

Cassandra's prophesies were doomed not to be believed and even the "river-wind draws a long sigh of disbelief," but Vincenz' readers are fortunate: his is a poetry of elegant hermeneutics, an ontological exploration as Vincenz is "on the search for stories of creation." He poses questions that expose inherited myth ("Why on earth / does life begin / with a single bright fruit?") and test our perceptions ("To watch a flower bloom / or a cloud fatten may be near impossible but how do you distinguish movement away or toward from the growth of billowing form?"). Yet the book is never ponderous, often humorous, eschewing what "sounds more or less like New Age claptrap." This is poetry that matters through its very quest for meaning: "Isn't there a potential for chaos in everything we see and touch? Where's the meaning in that?"

This tightly structured and imaginatively expansive work is akin to an Escher staircase, where laws of gravity are suspended so that we ascend and descend, holding the handrail of impeccable lines, stopping to stand in stanzas of timelessness, some of which lead "out of that honeycomb of life and enter that other world where there are no numbers to contain all of this." Vincenz reveals kairos within chronos and the "swathes of time steeped in eternity's teapot." Highly olfactory, from the realistic —"sweat, / perfume, fungal spores"— to the fantastic—"the fragrance of significant things / that appear to exist only in the mind, no more"—Vincenz follows his nose to the primordial source and we gladly follow him, even as we are impatient for more gnosis ("I know, I know, you want clarity, an illuminated mind, / not those fleeting visions of a future not yet born.") If death is the mother of beauty, then Vincenz fathers beauty further. With *Beautiful Rush*, he has achieved what "seems like immortality." This book is a must-read that must be read to be believed. If "to be outside of convention is the ticket," *Beautiful Rush* is a unique creation, a daring and gorgeously realized work, wherein "words are tuning forks ringing inside / glass minds." At times oracular, always spectacular, the beautiful words in *Beautiful Rush* will long resonate inside readers' minds.

– Kimberly L. Becker

Damn it!
What kind of evil, ripped-up animals we are!
Perhaps that's the reason every now and then
we do something quite beautiful.

—Alexander Xaver Gwerder (1923–1952)

Not the Last Word

Does the death
of a daughter

mean naught?
Genetics, simply a code?

Yes, I know, you've said
you taught yourself

to talk to flowers
and you're forever

forgetting our rainy summers—
and those container

travelers from the other side
of the globe,

now clumped together
in can't-swing-a-cat spaces

delineating
fortunate fashion brands

that keep you together,
as you wait for her

to arrive again—this time
with brilliant cat eyes.

CASSANDRA'S SMOKE

That foul breath of the city
waters the eye,

                but the nose,
self-assured, carries on—

embracing whatever
comes its way:

                sweat,
                        perfume,

fungal spores lofted over
mountain ranges

in puffed up storm clouds,

                jagged desert-dust,
bits of life dredged up.

                    Still,
the megaphone urges you to waltz
                to pass the long-short-long time

in a park,
                where old fools battle
                        crickets and compare
                        bird feathers,

where dogs shit and rut,
                where artists seek the ears

of trees and pansies

    and crumbling brick—

        but a riptide

of taxis and buses burns carbon dioxide

    through your arteries,

you hear voices

in hard labor,

    and behind closed rooms,

you hear something
        like knowledge,

            clearing its throat.

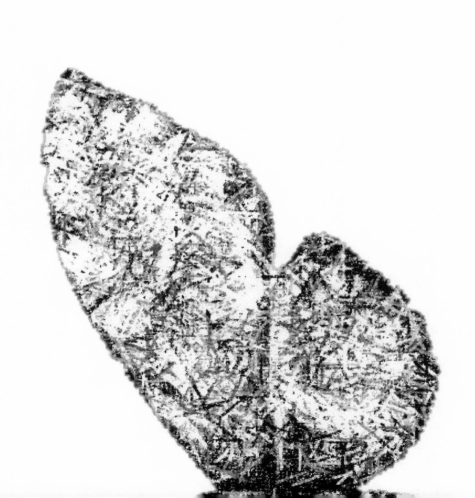

A Bitter Taste of Midnight

We all have our time machines, don't we.
Those that take us back are memories …
And those that carry us forward are dreams.

—H. G. Wells

BEAUTIFUL RUSH (I)

What time is it, my love?

Inexorable,

      this damned feeling,

nothing less than:

      all I know is

there is

      no morning,

and here

      in this frayed child's book,—

with that lord of time, H. G.—

      worlds collide

and words are

      tuning forks

          ringing inside

            glass minds.

O, to write an ode to Beauty,

       to write an ode at all,

but the exhausting grip

       of the handheld camera

and fingers twiddling

       plastic nodes,

the clicking—or the whorl

       of a painful Chinese brushstroke

with its double-signifiers

       of mountain and magic

and that leafed cadence of eloquent prayer

       hummed in stasis

in terse a cappella tones

       or perhaps a caterwaul of catcalls,

an *Om mani padme hum*

       or the Amen of *please please come back home*

and that wide-arched Olympian hurl

carrying its diurnal grays and this, this

lonely whitish-haze morning thrusts

    into long gravelly afternoons.

What then *is* your final opiate of choice?

    is it perhaps those coins burning up wishes in wells?

or the greening of oval cells

    scraping silently together like coins themselves,

falling upon each other in oxidized dust

    and that ecstatic worm of science segmenting itself,

twisting upon the base prime

    or perhaps it's light pixelating in light

upon light within Rømer's long-light-time—

    and at night, the silent grave-digging

for antediluvian bones, for crude evidence

    of concerned mammals,

or the brittle souls of saints

and those unrepeating,

unrepeating worlds?

or does the eye meet something else

entirely inhuman, entirely unheard of?

SMALL CHANGE

You're ready to pop your first.

He looks twice
as if he might remember me. Damn,
you were a siren that day in the warm grass,
butterflies slipping in and out
of your red-gold hair
and the taste of you
like 5 grams of codeine
in the burnish of late afternoon.

Across the Thames, river-wind
draws a long sigh of disbelief.

These constant farewells
in God's less profound light,
the evening's last tango and that riffle
of taffeta bearing down upon visceral dust.

Last prelude to midsummer sex
and the breath of late morning.

The days blur.

Only later you register that twinge
in a strange bare room
in a trance from the night before.

CASSANDRA'S DEAD WANTS

inspired reverence
not just rebellion.

And who was that grim figure
who left the running of the house
to her girls?

Saul adored her,
but like the others, found her
quite bewildering.

As if in reading aloud
words might become
symbols of need,

as if in years,
time became

entirely
irrelevant.

Affection came only
when age regressed
into childhood again.

The taking out
of one daughter
might not leave
a permanent stillness.

The taking in of another
abated in the mind's eye.

The vast veiled mystery
entitled her to tie
her bonds of logic.

And to astonish
with single words

is all she could
truly wish for

when real life
is all there really was.

BEAUTIFUL RUSH (II)

And suddenly the drunken voice blathers: "Reach in,"

    and repeats, "Reach in."

To what, I ask you, to what?

    An inner being? an inner-self outwardly exposed?

Sounds more or less like New Age claptrap.

    I know I think I know.

This nuanced, numbered man dares *hello*.

    Hello, hot fingers moving fast.

Just who is this guru

    who dares declare the blatant?

"Wrap it all up in a see-thru blanket," he chuckles.

    "One you've slept and cursed in for weeks," he says.

"One that's falling into rags, almost.

    Then let the whole caboodle loose

upon a river that rides

    into skin-tearing waterfalls,

upon the ever-becoming,

      the whirring of thoughts beading."

And when I think I know I know,

      he says: "Observe carefully!

                        Watch, you fool, watch!"

and eyes roll wide-eyed as if in mock amusement,

      but more like a preying bird's—

or so it seems—as the tourists

      gobble up all my woes,

and those fresh green mangoes

      with their sour-sweet—

and somewhat akin to warts, those crab-apples

      tumble out of my nose.

I become a whiff of spice bazaar myself,

      as I've done before—the fragrance

of significant things

      that appear to exist

only in the mind, no more—

       there's that purifying myrrh

and her sister frankincense—

       and may all three kings kneel down

before him as once they did before—

       or at least two of the three

that kickstarted our child-

       upon-a-star shopping spree—

AN ABUNDANCE OF ISLANDS

Swaths of time steeped in eternity's teapot.
Desolate wonder of infinite space—your face
in my hands, growing old, your fingers along

the bend of my spine, your nose, your fabulous
freckled nose. The river wandering, the sea an island,
the land a sea. The interdependency of chance

events—a language called stillness, a child
called language. Grandfather's war scars.
Mother's tuberculosis—coughing at the edge

of the bed, a jackknife, stray sock, a cup
of ice cold tea. Lemon rind. And she, paper,
the ancient carbon backbone crumpled.

You say: *but don't souls return to the mountain—*
walk leaf-littered paths through the forest of the living?
The dead, of course, shuffle paved roads,

endless highways, strafe deserts, molten rock.
But how do you warm the departed?
With broken bread and communion, my love.

With the blood of wilderness—& wind.
Or not,
or not.

Simenon's Cultural Misfortune

In non-being
I coveted being,
in being, I coveted
love. Perhaps
that's why I could never
turn out the light
on the wilderness
of our future.

The words
of the day swerve
like the shell
of a sideways-
scurrying
crustacean snagged
on another Buddha's
barbed tongue.

BEAUTIFUL RUSH (III)

Balls-free-

      British-bollocks nude,

this fakir milk-drawing—

      and would you believe—

straight into his member of members,

      his personal snake lunging

in the milking bowl, a technique

      supposedly applied since the Punic Wars.

"That's holy milk," he says, smiling.

      And it's one of those smiles

that's cut by an izmel, not in a synagogue,

      not in a mosque, but in a saint's chapel.

"And we're not outnumbered," he says.

      "We're far too old."

And yet, your hair still cascades

into both of our eyes

like hay, like Arabian horsetails.

But like my Royal Air Force granddad,

did you ever learn

to iron your own clothes?

cut creases with hot iron and coal?

"Let it pour," he says.

Let me guess—

like holy milk?

And then he really takes it beyond a canter,

spitting and lunging, heaving into himself

like a draft horse, Shropshire or Clydesdale:

"In five full moons a dove shall appear—

the ghost of someone

you once held chest-close."

Who did he think he was? fucking Nostradamus?

But how to explain that bird twittering

right up in my ear, up close. On the other hoe,

it was like a nagging, a horse-nagging

without perfunctory words. You were good at that.

That horsey nibbling.

You were good at most things.

Even the wiggling of toes.

Wishing I had been. Wishing I was.

And in that wishing for, that I was.

With all the goddamn soldiering on,

you forgot the clichés.

Like those cheap pink sunglasses you once wore

upon your upturned nose

that offered no UV protection at all.

Come closer, come close, dear.

Let me breathe into your ear.

But really, your fingertip is what I pine for,

tracing my skin like forever-beach sand—

And, truly, no, truly, I wonder what she draws?

By the way, what time is it now, love?

.

CASSANDRA'S DESIGNATED LIGHT

Isn't there a potential for chaos
in everything we see and touch?
Where's the meaning in that?

If being is just listening
did I finish knowing, then?
To be outside of convention
is the ticket, not an image
one might envision
upon a crinkled page.

Who is the patriarch?
and who the master?
the I in her?
And who the sky
that hangs above,
blue and in its foul temper?

And those ragged novels
of romance and crime,
easy to read,
infused
with nothing
but a designated light.

Didn't Mother once say
we can become
anything we want?

A Bitter Taste of Midnight

The song of the world.

    The bones of folklore.

        The resonance of reality.

            The rapture of being alive.

                The meaning of a flower.

                    The meaning of a flea.

                        A moth without a light blub.

                          An aphid without a rose.

                    What can't be known,

and then,
walking into that cave,

placing your mind square
in the middle
of those temporal aberrations

in sight of duality.
It all starts with sin, and then,
everything with difference

is a fall from grace.
O, to be in a place
where no one ever heard

of that 'wickedness.'
To be on the search
for stories of creation

and finding
a vast underground
of pure silence.

Why on earth
does life begin
with a single bright fruit?

The snake sheds its skin
as the moon
sheds its shadow.

I say:
kiss the cobra
square on the nose.

VOICES BREAKING

As the world, if it is matter,
Is impenetrable.

—George Oppen, *Of Being Numerous*

Beautiful Rush (IV)

Nothing more than the tomb:

  Tutankhamen and his gilded corpse,

a masked reliquary of stares and that pose,

  those lifetime-leaning stances

upon the pedestal and a serpentine rod

  scratching an itch

upon a regal calf,

  nothing more.

"Observe the dove dance

  over the mountain, the lightning

your little old grandmother's

  bioluminescent ghost!"

She, arms wide as wings,

  she who talked of flight

as if she had a bird's-eyed clue.

Oh yes, she knew: swallows,

bats, bumblebees, befriended

stallions, serpents,

iridescent caterpillars,

incandescent worms.

My, my, what a woman of the wild world!—

I know, I know.

Hot fingers move fast.

Upon the squeegee breasts

of all the blossoming girls.

Ears open, I wanted so much to listen.

Eyes closed, I wanted so far to see

that fleck of pure white, a flock of birds

upon the horizon's expression,

an umlaut

over an unending sea—

and was there a cedilla

baited somewhere beneath?

I'd like to think so—

To Watch a Flower Bloom

Can the known world be mapped
across the knotted surface of the brain
with nothing more than a compass and a plumb line?

He knows toe movements are restricted
to the confines of a shoe.

Are we simply to multiply
clues as on an abacus or a slide rule?

In the fine-toothed comb of perception,
the judgment
invariably cascades into ambiguity
as the axis mundi shifts
into its next reincarnation.

To watch a flower bloom
or a cloud fatten may be nearly impossible

but how *do* you distinguish movement away
from or toward the growth of billowing form?

not just that slice of buttered toast or the definition
of light in shadow, in broccoli,

in the sinuous threads
of musculature beneath those layers of fat,

but the association of other
cognitive or ruddy stimulators

color-numbering the ever-present electro-
magnetism and those sonic vibrations outside

that snow-globe of volition
and that goddamnit goddamnit

vile fear
of the tart tang of social recognition.

Even in a million years, he'll never master that foxtrot,

it smells far too much
like he doesn't own himself.

WITH ORWELL IN HIS EAR
SIMENON CONSIDERS CASSANDRA'S HEARING

My initial concern
is to get a hearing.
No parting line
but a searing eye.
If there's hope
it lies in the masses.
What is under-
neath, though?
What's it like
to be the victim?
Bound up
with solid breakfasts
and gloomy Sundays,
the yellow mailboxes
have entered your soul—
where once
your voice yearned,
your heart still sings.
More rubbish
from heaven.
Hearing?
Nothing.

ALMOST TAX FREE

And silver the tears,
the Moon's harrowed lament—
she who had once loved
immeasurably. "Money,"
Uncle Fortunato said,
"is portable power—
why else do we *In God Trust*?
The word *credit* comes from 'crede,'—
to believe. I know from experience: to be happy
with money is to be fanatically blind."

People asked me over there
on the other side
of the world, What's your interest?
Are you creditworthy?
Have you had your neck
dragged down
with bulging silver purses,
been prodded
with a loan shark's knife?
And did I know those sweet
medieval Florentines paid for everything
in oranges so artists could inspire beauty.

Whispering, they suggested
I maintain a second book,
a ledger where transnational
mysteries might be captured. "In the end,"
they said, "the damned
become divinities." "And who," they said,

"doesn't think they were smarter than
the ones that came before?"

And: "Isn't every empire
built on borrowed money"; or,
"where the hell do you find,
that transcendental subprime?

                              "The euthanasia
of the bondholder is the drug of the
government, surely."

So I asked them: was this the new world
we wore as daisies woven in our hair
when we were Summer's children,
that land beyond the dreams of avarice?

"You've hit the mother lode," they said—
"it all follows a steep bell-curve.

"Surely you know you dwell
in the dustbin of new prosperity?"

Beautiful Rush (V)

and the sun fingering

      crowns of trees as if, as if,

they were the unkempt mops

      of adolescent boys, but when

that bundled blanket burst, well—

      and the nuanced mangoes and

those crab-apples of misfortune,

      not the golden ones of the sun

as W. B. saw them, you know,

      but those below, tumbling like pitted rocks,

crackling with their pips and frothing

      from the horse's well-chewed bit—

O Calcutta of the glass mind,

      misfortune hit the water like skipping stones

and this large, dour four-eyed fish

(two spying above, two search-and-destroying below),

sprung up with its quivering gonopodium, straight

from its own ocean wishing well and snapped, snapped

straight through that corded rope

binding it all together—

even you, you who drew

Tutankhamen's billowing breath,

even you, who drew *his* tomb upon my chest

from mole to mole, from truss to trestle, and treasured me up

in your ancient womb

of unspoken words,

but it didn't matter at all.

—"Says who?"

He's about to spout again

like a hot-nozzled Szechuan teapot

into his seven-wondered world—

Oh no, holy shit. Here he comes

with all that holy milk.

"One lump or two?"

Light it up, will you.

Caruso sings for us all.

Yes, I know you do.

The scorpion on her shoulder blade,

the worm lodged under her impeccable arched sole.

Where was my temple of restraint?

For now I flex my rose,

and the flies, those ankle-pestering flies—

for now, a peach-and-velvet-petal road.

CASSANDRA'S LEVELHEADED COMPANY

Knowing the stars
gave her a sense
of reality.

Knowing less
than what she knew
others had, gave her
a sense of place.

She needed means
to believe
and to doubt.

And through a riddle
when in doubt,
when standing alone

at rebellion,
even careless
wisdom had to go.

To be one
of the lingering
'wicked' ones,

to be sealed
in an icy fate.

What is it really
to be honest?

I choose
what governs
the syntax
within this level-headed
company.

She, at Heart, a Blue Whale

(1)

not only in our blood, but in theirs—

ocean trenches fathoms deep, where no hand
has swept—

Murmuring`
ancient bone music,
skin songs
and marrowed incantations.

Radiation, of course,
is a speck in the eye.

And what is the particle's
smallest participle?

Isn't it one within another,
that blood and skin and cartilage and bone?

More then than water lessons, then?

Something, perhaps, to do with the birthing of suns?

(2)

awaken, dear monster and take us in,

for on that day over 1000 dolls arrived, porcelain-
perfect blue-eyed dolls, yet cracked and chipped
and stressed like any icon under pressure;
1000 serpents followed, figures weighing in
success and ambition, shedding outer layers in ribbons;
and we men, we men, belly-up in the sand, staring
dreamlessly at a blue sky, but then, seeing fortuitous signals:
fruiting trees and swallows arrowing in pairs—
yet it all ended in the dolls' eyes.

Isn't that where you read the soul?

(3)

and not a single elegiac tone,

but the centrifugal force was a man on a lake
swallowing demons. He smoked a pipe stuffed with cinnamon
and Indian tobacco. We, in need of air, lived on breathing.

And the sky, in its shimmering gold was taunting us to fly
and those bicycles wheeled to their end—which again
was a numbered thing—enumerated and tired.

"We had long forgotten the last revolution
and the bees, their legs pollen-less,
were scrounging dregs of sugared paper wrappers
making a honeycomb in glowing red and green and neon blue."

He spoke of an emperor's trundling wheel, and then said:

"And thus, the world expands again—
O those lungs breathing in the primitive force of future
are hallowed in the word of a distant past."

Isn't there another word for belonging?

(4)

and now, climb into the view:

the window inside shimmers
yet outside
nothing is bright.

I'm swollen from a night
of excess

and time has slowed down
to a thump

in the root
of my neck.

Is this the world I've come to know
on the back of my hand?

How to Die of Beauty

Tread softly because you tread on my dreams.

—W. B. Yeats, *The Wind Among the Reeds*

Simenon's Speck of Gladness

when the sea

        shakes the walls

and an infinity

of ghostly shoes   lines blue-eyed

towns

    where I am   not yet dead

      where

I am not quite

born

You Who Were Once More Raconteur than Rebel,

more cardiologist

than card shark.
And,
drowning

in your eyes,
three flies born

the day before upon the molding
bread of grim
heat.

Do you recall
where evenings went

when we drew short straws

when there was always a good
decision
since revolution
followed everything else,

when the land cooled
to a steely glint

or the sea pressing against
our hardy shores

barely scratched the surface?

Have your lips gone dry of tales?

Is there nothing left of your dreams at all?

REMBRANDT'S LAST FRUIT

'Course you'd like to ask God how long
it took him to build an apple, and
if the first was red or green, if it fit
in the heart of the palm between
the lifeline and the mind
and if there were snapshots
of that first crunch—perhaps he'd say
each was a masterpiece, each perfect
and spectacularly flawed and every single seed
conveniently inserted by children's fingers.

'Course you'd like to know what the devil said:
something about the seed being more than a metaphor—
we all know it's easier to build
an empire with many little fingers.
God may be the eye of geometry,
but isn't it still boggling how apples
have spread across the globe, lending
power and meaning to what is yet to come?
Surely the soul of a woman
is the sum of all her walks,
so I ask you, what can enlighten a life
any more than a pair of sturdy shoes?

BEAUTIFUL RUSH (VI)

O glitter

    of my dying star.

O glittering

    world beyond my oyster.

Your clamshell, a buttercup.

    In your hand a simple daisy grows—somehow.

Between your taxpaying cracks in those roadworks.

    I know I know I think.

Would you tell me, my love.
    What is time at all?

But she says *scatter*:

     let the sand rush into our eyes

and may the night, the night, remain embedded

     in our splintered bones—

Oh, those vitreous reflections

     of our personal ghosts.

"Blah," he says. "Pooh pooh," he says.

     "Give her that fucking precious rose.

You know nothing of nature,

     nothing of blossoming beauty

or that fanciful truth.

     Let her be the one.

Let her be the one

     the gods choose."

STANZAS IN LOVE WITH THEMSELVES

Relinquished
in this image—

once visceral,
now just a word—

a matins-ringing
of church bells

and those Catholics
to and fro

in supplicant-heavy hands,
the throbbing, a yearning

for non-damnation,
for damned epiphany;

and that ephemeral
glazed-over glance

as lover to lover,
nose upon broken nose,

but staring, staring
into vast distances

and smoking out
the origin of stars.

Beyond. Facing
the Wailing Wall

a love-pure *mechitza*,
a trembling matchmaking,

core within core
finger-warming

the hand, a heart pulsing
precariously, feeding

that deep dark,
that dark-deep,

forever-dying
universal seething.

THE INNER EYE TATTOOED

(1)

Looking in
like a snail,

my nose crawls
against glass.

How the view
alters up close

and the breath
a mountainous fog

against matter's
impermeable will.

Isn't this the color
of pure silence—

that rainbowed tint
when night swallows reflections?

(2)

In the nothingness
of the primordial,

words written before
words are known

and the constellations,
planetoid hope,

stars flush against
the skin of a peeled eye—

a stalking with inner
meaning rewritten

in paper, on wood,
carved in stone,

rewritten for a cavern
of gnawed bone,

fragments scattered
in a semblance of home.

(3)

O to breathe in
that dust, to test

the synapses with
potential meaning:

a gun barrel, a gin bottle,
a diode, vermouth, a grenade—

and at a ray's knifepoint
within night this moronic

light cutting deep
into the gilded dome.

Civilizations compounded
in the chicken-gut of divinations.

And that round pill
of morning purpled

in the royal cloak
of an inevitable twilight:

that mad aerial dance
of sparrows beyond

our crinkled
silver lining.

(4)

You know there's fishbone
caught in your throat

and that grope, the hair-
ruffle of aunts and uncles.

And behind, flickering,
a predator stalking,

the TV-eyes of the dark—
words holding out,

words clinging on,
gathering in formulations

congregating in clarified
intentions of rice

and straw and wildflowers—
the storm's plague above,

balling grey and black and
something pterodactyl-winged

like a fire dragon.
And how within the click

and crackle of strip lighting, you
creature-sensation, you bloom

upon the aphid's abdomen.
Are there words enough?

Is there blood enough
to bleed

while crouching
at the on/off button?

(5)

O the words for this.
Those pulsing veins of lust,

the seven severed heads
of that mythological canine,

fishes swimming through a murk
of clogged arteries, your innocent eyes

and the stressed follicles
of your feline fur, the marvels

beyond time straight
into the face

of a dimmed
inarticulate world.

(6)

I know, I know,
you want clarity,

an illuminated mind,
not those fleeting visions

of a future not yet born.
You want it all inked,

a universe out-worldly
branded in the foundry,

the blast furnace
of structure in the making

and that tremolo of voices
slowly breaking.

DAMAGED MUSIC

Ache in the old wisdom tooth,
an experience of self-fulfilling

prophesy, a damaged magic
and acres of elephant bones.

Here we go: Another evening
of cold fiction, the starved

ghosts of ancient citadels.
I wish I might breathe sparrows

into the sky or wind-weather
the wild grass. I yearn

for the smell of the day
in spring, for a language

without words. May I
one day climb out

of that honeycomb of life
and enter that other world

where there are no numbers
to contain all of this, and

the smooth bloody
thickness of oil flows

into the smut
of an ever-endless night.

THE FORKED FINGER SHRIVELS

"A word to the wise," it says.
"Open your mind.
The cold words

will return to enfold you
in the bittersweet love
of melting ice.

Let those silent epiphanies
of ragged passion sear
under your hot skin."

Cassandra Knows How to Die of Beauty

Who knows
what it's like to be dead

when we incessantly chatter
between rooms?

The name, love,
is crossed out.

O to write
letter after letter

belaboring
a fruitless cause.

A letter, of course,
seems like immortality.

NOTES

"Small Change" is after August Kleinzahler.

"A Bitter Taste of Midnight" is for Joseph Campbell.

"Almost Tax Free" is for the city of Zug, Switzerland.

"Rembrandt's Last Fruit" is for Katia Kapovich.

"Cassandra Knows How to Die of Beauty" is after Emily Dickinson.

AFTERWORD

"What is it really to be honest?" And why would we really *be* honest? To root in a particular geography of self at the same time as proposing more macro geographies in which the particulars of others can roost? For the sake of *time seeking real time* by way of sensory stories, by "words as tuning forks," by briny rhymes?

Are some people's poems sacred scars? Marks of the page as quirks in a day, as scratches into the body for meaning? Etches in a headboard. Drag marks from outstretched finger along a foggy window ("where I am not yet dead/where I am not quite born"). Curls made in hair ("your hair still cascades in both of our eyes"). Cracks made in the counter from slamming down a dish. Sneaker streaks pushed into the mud.

Who watches as our days pass us by? "Bioluminescent ghost[s]?" Who notices when we get caught in the crannies of the quotidian? And who etches into their own forms for retention, in acknowledgement of us, when those catches of many types present as beauty?

Vincenz' *Beautiful Rush* is a belaboring of the details of daily life in an effort at synthesizing them *for* beauty, *from* cliché. It is hard to live. It is hard to write living. Why then are we pulled to write it? What are we hoping to contact? What is worth this effort?

Vincenz' "intentional concern is to get a hearing," to hit the "mother lode:" a place where the wealth of somatic resonances can exist, can thrive even while cancelling certain things out. Where "hot fingers move fast," the "Buddha's barbed tongue" is eating out "the I in her." By "damaged magic" "the snake sheds its skin as the moon sheds its shadow." Led by sweat and perfume, by the foulness of the city "where artists seek the ears," we encounter the slow motility of days as they attends to figures, are attended to and brought near by certain attentions.

Reincarnation, melancholy, meals, small deaths, "eloquent prayers," "silent grave digging," this book rings with the most human of poems. I define a human poem, as a poem that "hear[s] voices in hard labor," that can admit its kinship to various shortcomings, needs for anesthetic. Human poems are poems capable of working with their *imagined others* wherein something/ entirely inhuman, entirely unheard of," can be met, reckoned with. For what is it to be human, beyond the seeking out of home? Beyond "a language called stillness, a child called language?"

The umlaut, in its subtle morphology, reveals roots: the secret (sacred) lives of our body parts in tandem, in multiplicity as they animate our bodies. "There is no morning," and the "frayed child's book" is flipping us as travelers, through personal names, personal moments ("your face in my hands growing old"). "I'm swollen from [this] excess," just as I had hoped to be: calm as I die in small bits every day. There is a pristine fulfillment in dying like this, alongside the language: its lips, the rips, so many riffs.

– j/j hastain

ACKNOWLEDGEMENTS

"An Abundance of Islands," "Cassandra's Smoke," and "Almost Tax Free" previously appeared in *Battersea Review*.

An excerpt of "Beautiful Rush (i)" previously appeared in *Star*Line*.

"Cassandra's Levelheaded Company," "She, at Heart, a Blue Whale," "Stanzas in Love with Themselves," and "Rembrandt's Last Fruit" previously appeared in *Superstition Review*.

"The Inner Eye Tattooed" previously appeared in *Heavy Feather Review*.

About the Author

Marc Vincenz is British-Swiss, was born in Hong Kong, and has published five previous collections of poetry: *The Propaganda Factory, or Speaking of Trees; Gods of a Ransacked Century, Mao's Mole, Behind the Wall at the Sugar Works* (a verse novel) and *Additional Breathing Exercises* (bilingual German-English). His chapbooks are *Benny and the Scottish Blues, Genetic Fires, Upholding Half the Sky* and *Pull of the Gravitons*.

He is also the translator of numerous German-language poets, including: Erika Burkart, Ernst Halter, Klaus Merz, Andreas Neeser, Markus Bundi and Alexander Xaver Gwerder. His translation of Alexander Xaver Gwerder's selected poems, *Casting a Spell in Spring,* is to be released by Coeur Publishing in late 2014. He has edited various anthologies and selected works of other poets, including Hugh Fox's last and posthumous collection, *Primate Fox.* He has received grants from the Swiss Arts Council, ProHelvetia, for his translations and a fellowship from the Literary Colloquium Berlin (LCB). His work has been translated into German, Russian, Romanian and French.

Marc is the publisher and executive editor of MadHat Press, *MadHat Annual* (formerly *Mad Hatters' Review*) and *MadHat Lit.* He is Coeditor-in-Chief of *Fulcrum: An Anthology of Poetry and Aesthetics,* and serves on the editorial board of *Open Letters Monthly.* He is also Director of Evolution Arts, Inc, a non-profit organization that promotes independent presses and journals.

OTHER BOOKS BY MARC VINCENZ

The Propaganda Factory, or Speaking of Trees

Gods of a Ransacked Century

Mao's Mole

Behind the Wall at the Sugar Works (a verse novel)

Additional Breathing Exercises (bilingual German-English selected poems)

This Wasted Land and Its Chymical Illuminations (annotated by Tom Bradley)

Translations:

Kissing Nests (translations of Werner Lutz)

Nightshift / An Area of Shadows (translations of Erika Burkart and Ernst Halter)

Grass Grows Inward (translations of Andreas Neeser)

Out of the Dust (translations of Klaus Merz)

10396609R00064

Made in the USA
San Bernardino, CA
13 April 2014